By Some Happenstance

also by Dominic Albanese
Notebook Poems
Bastards Had the Whole Hill Mined
Iconic Whispers
Then-n-Now
Love Is Not Just a Word (with Seb Doubinsky)
Only the River Knows
The Wizard & the Wrench (with Ambika Devi)
Boardwalk Dreams
Midway Moves
Disconnected Memories

By Some Happenstance

Dominic Albanese

©2019 Dominic Albanese

book design and layout: SpiNDec, Port Saint Lucie, FL
cover image: *Bear Point, 2018* Kris Haggblom

All rights reserved.

  No part of this book may be used or reproduced in any manner whatsoever without written permission except in the case of brief quotations embodied in critical articles and reviews. Members of educational institutions and organizations wishing to photocopy any of the work for classroom use, or authors, artists and publishers who would like to obtain permission for any material in the work, should contact the publisher.

Printed in the United States of America.

Published by Poetic Justice Books
Port Saint Lucie, Florida
www.poeticjusticebooks.com

ISBN: 978-1-950433-00-1

FIRST EDITION
10 9 8 7 6 5 4 3 2 1

praise for Dominic Albanese's poetry:

Richard Spisak: *A fine poet who soars and dives and wrings from a colorful life the true ore of wonder...*

Alicia Neville: *You write what you are... brutal, beautiful, bounteous.*

Michael Brown: *You earned your double urned burned cup of unnatural brew on this one!*

Ani Hurley: *Good Lordy, you do have a way with the words ...*

Christina Quinn: *[Dominic's] poems give me sweet dreams.*

Matt Borczon: *Perfect!! Every needed word!*

Donna-Lee Phillips: *Amen again. I like who you are now... what is more important is that YOU like who you are. Very powerful!!*

Andrew Vachss: *Takes guts to go that route, [but Dominic's] never had a shortage of that commodity.*

Michael Sedano: *People who read poetry, who seek commanding expression and arresting ideas, will tell their friends to order the collection...*

Sonja Mongar: *The best thing about listening to Dominic read is that he's such a fabulous, engaging storyteller. Someone should follow him around with a tape recorder!*

Aureleo Rosano: *BRAVO, BRAVO. Never stop writing. It is your gift to civilization ... and a fine one at that.*

First and foremost, to all who have read and made mention of my books. Every one of you, fellow poets, pals, lovers and friends. I can not make a list for fear I leave out some one who has helped me called me on my failings and been there for me and believed in me when I had a hard time believing in myself. We all shine on, every one of us, some on paper some on canvas, some sit still looking out a window, watching traffic go by.

In loving memory of Maddy Madison and Spain Rodriquez, who were real brothers to me, while my real brothers were out of touch. I dedicate this book to my Brothers now gone Thomas Dennis and Robert Walter Albanese.....and my Parents Patsy and Mary...may they all rest and know I carry on.

By Some Happenstance

Dominic Albanese

contents
1 I Suppose
2 *poem by poem*
3 *been so long*
4 *wait, for a few more hours*
5 *the meaning of poetry*
6 *close your eyes*
7 *go / you are still*
8 *when / and / if*
9 *where are the women*
10 *let me ask myself this question*
11 *there are visions*
12 *one repeat*
13 *I must confess*
14 *there was a*
15 *bernal heights*
16 *driving in night traffic*
17 *grown up poems*
18 *cross over october*
19 *cooking / doing homework*
20 *what words*
21 *well / I already seen*
22 *somehow / in spite of all*
23 *who will hold me*
24 Mid Night

25 New York Times
26 Escape Road
28 Bicycle Poem
29 Person or Person's Unknown
30 Close No Cigar
31 Penny Wise
32 Symptoms
33 When
34 Broadway (frisco) 210 am (1)
35 Broadway (frisco) 210 am (2)
36 Here It Is this Cold...
38 Folsom Dam
39 Gone Starker
40 Monastic
41 La Gloria
42 Thinking Again
43 Subway Cars
44 Grumpy
45 To Cook a Pot of Rice
46 *the sameness of the days*
47 *I wonder if*
48 *o dear*
49 *last year I crossed a line*
50 *with one breath I tell*
51 *had to cry out*
52 *miscreants malefactors muggers*
53 *who will lay a flower*
54 *anyone reading*

55 *out night walking again*
56 *opium in bed*
57 *soon another calendar*
58 *don't have enough days left*
59 *can't seem to trust a lot*
60 *all the effort*
61 *words escape*
62 *out alone*
63 *we will see what*
64 *what it seems like*
65 *got a good job*
66 *the night demons still*
67 *when this batch*
68 *in the space of one week*
69 *Monday evening*
70 *this will not*
71 *better take refuge*
72 *demons depart*
73 *at risk again*
74 *walk by the church*
75 *was I bored*
76 *return of the smiley eyed...*
77 *did I really*
78 *the rose / of gerke alley*
79 *believe it*
80 By Some Happenstance

By Some Happenstance

I Suppose

sitting here another hour
jaw jacking in comments
or pass by some click bait
or
an adorable cat video
might not subtract that
eventual toll of days...we all get
how ever..with 14 reels in one box
and 11 in another....all needing the administrating
deft touch of these talented phalanges
earning as it were...my daily bread
I bid the page adieu
and go
bout what I need
to
If I am to sustain as it were
the terrible habit I have
of
wanting enough to eat....and pay my bills
cheerfully and with no rancor
or well....I just do the best I can
hiss mutter n spit
at recalcitrant parts
strip em soak em
lube em and put em back
to good working order
flash dash with a bit
o my special lube cover
shiny n new
what else can a poor boy
do

poem by poem
page by page
I scribble
these words alone
tonight I told
some one
poetry
unlike auto repair
has no specs
no rules
boundary lines
are empty lines
lines not yet
written
poem by poem
page by page

been so long
since I wrote
anyone
a letter
wouldn't know where
it is alone
I sit
talking to the computer
snatching the words
from nowhere
intended for anyone
bopping by

the people I know
are unaware
that I sit alone
writing
it is a secret of mine

these poems are letters
addressed to whom it may concern
general statements about life
the hereafter
the things that puzzle me
feelings I have
and can't talk about
not from shame
but from ignorance
or unwillingness

take a chance
I tell myself over and over
do this
because

wait, for a few more hours
do what you can
           to not completely fall apart
this is the only chance at real solid
steady paychecks you have left

if this goes up in dust, you are done
no part of any other option is open
for just a few more years
             endure the garage
                  hours needed to get security
do you really think you can live in this shack
and eat acorns
do you have some idea what it's going to be like
to be seventy
             with no place warm or safe
             to lay down in
are you aware of how close to final self destruct
this last few weeks have been
                  who, do you think does not wonder
is he sick
or on some shit showing the true face
of pain

    the meaning of poetry
is not clear to me
I seek bodies
minds
attention
with words on paper
emotions
ideas fantasy
fiction personal fact
almost any thing goes
in the style I chose
    as I write to no one person
or all who listen
or hear

close your eyes
    do not cry
the orchid lily
    did not die
the rose
    still hides
  among the thorns
time of day
yet unborn
     o sleep
      my lady
I am here
this is but
another year

go
you are still
young
there are
alleyways
    doorways
    big houses
little windows
all sorts of persons
places unknown
there is
the real
the almost real
it will all end

the rain
the horizon
the keys
to the locks
all the known
the not yet discovered

when
    and
        if
I see that redhead again
i'd say very softly
in voice music
your face
it's here in my
memory forever
it comes up every day
loud and clear
the sight of you
in passing
is inside my soul
the way she walked
was all I needed
if she says
anything
i'll kiss her

where are the
women
the ones I knew
for whatever length of time
memories of scents linger
faces dissolve reappear
dresses, scarves, shoes
dressed up
or
naked

focus slow motion
one gets on a bus
the other just departs
places faces
past present future
in daylight
or shadow

where are the
women
the ones I knew
for what ever length of time

a kiss
for them all
now
then
later
here
or in passing
did I ever know
them
at all

let me ask myself this question,
    (is that not what poets do)
    why
don't I write, what keeps me from saying, what I see
even in the everyday of things, some so simple, like starlight
some so complex, like river current.

days o days go by, work, food, foolish novels
    all distract
    all detract
    all deter
this life on tracks, a runaway train, me aboard
waiting for words to come into the station
get up off the bench,

there are visions
in the night
painted face
gauze dress skirt billow
motor cycle wind
    no magic women
        for me
long time now

one repeat
    encore
on broadway
in neon
and sidewalk
in asphalt
in steel
another window
watcher
another night
without sleeping
a late august
repartee
a summit
self inspection
sounding stone

the air on muni pier
at 6am
in gold foil
silk supported
say no more
    say no more

I must confess
    it took all my self control
not to burn the wedding album
      in the fireplace
the day I took my last few
things from her house

all I have with parting, bad
bitter memories
wasted submission, enduring every last
judgement, over and over, never good enough
sour, scolding, all in a voice so easy to listen to
even if it took all my power not to drop the bitch in
   her tracks
how did I get so
taken
why I did not get gone sooner

well it took my best attempt at stability
upended
I guess I am glad I did not burn it

there was a
girl named pamela pierce
in third grade
at cure of ars
a dominican catholic school

who wore a green jumper
   tan blouse
      white socks
saddle shoes

the one or two times
most I dared
let our eyes meet
I was devastated
totally undone

now some 40 years later
ima gotta irish sweetheart
who does the same sensation
up and down all over again

then
as now
I can only
wonder

bernal heights
   stone
   behind elsie street
at twilight
because of spring
orange glow
       shadow
dark figures of
trees
leaves floating
   safe for the
 simple
we sit
to pray
a bench at our feet
yellow flowers

    driving in night traffic, past
the happy new fortune café
    demolition teams gut an abandoned school
red light stop light head light brake light
passing in night traffic

closer to home, the sportsmen's outlet,
stuffed fish, sharp knives, hiking boots
more familiar landscape
    I am alone
as I have been for a year now

closed up stores, drive in grease pits
full of left over dead cow patties rancid fries
a small oil leak in my motor, stinks

approaching home, I laugh
the new happy fortune café
indeed

grown up poems
not the self absorbed pity moan of youth
unsure stutter voice about love
or the lack of it

no
these are more about life
here
and passing
the days the months the years

I read somewhere there are more signs than trees
in America
traffic signs
food signs
buy this buy that
signs
what is said
to those seeing
or those unseeing going by

grown up poetry
nothing to sell
nothing to buy
my own record
I love this country
sign the next sign I see
do this
in remembrance of
me

this grown up stuff
is what I feel not just what I see
quarter after five dark out
first day of December

cross over
        october
into winter
november
and the wind
      scorpio wind
over
clear chilly water
    as we grow
      older
one year older
      gifted
with time
nature changes
while most everything

dies
in order   (summer in limbo)

the first signs
snowfall
up on the mountain

cooking
doing homework
saving the world one sentence at a time
fun house
peep show
someone's little girl
turning tricks to get high

after all the pain
there is so little gain
night time streets neon rainbow
alley way of discarded dreams
empty taxi cabs off duty lights
reflected
storefront window dummy's waving good bye

what words
            prayers, poem lines
appear on the empty page
            could explain
internally, the overwhelming
            self hatred
leading me on this
road less end less
pathway of
            destruction
where is all the
            step by step
daily dispensation
years of attending
along side other tragic
addicts, drunk
defect laden
others
when will this long backward
death march be over
why, alone
            surrounded by
negative repeated
self induced agony
do I keep going
nowhere

well
I already seen
I can write here
under your roof
in your circle
so I don't gotta
nightwalk
or keep a kitchen table
somewhere separate

also did notice
oregon is sure quiet
like sleepy hollow
I been in concrete
sidewalk metal
traffic echos so long
here it don't need to be 4 am or later
here in your house
I seem safe
   or sitting still
anyway

somehow
　　in spite of all
　　the civil engineers
　　land fill
　　consultants
assorted assholes
public and private
equally greedy
tule grass marsh
has resurfaced
south of market
clara alley

who will hold me
in this empty night
as the crash descends
where is comfort
in all the shame
so classic
a stumble
out, up, frenzied
               foolish
all this has
been is some place
inside me one place or another
once said
    I don't care
the past efforts the foundation
has no grip
the worst of my persona
meets up with
my face of evil
wary walking in and out
of shadows
signs, neon reminders
death's head reflections
going by darkened windows

Mid Night

then I go
    to bed
having claimed
    this hour
to myself

word or two
    out loud
silent
reason it out

remember
    (the rule)
the show must
go on

New York Times

night
    tell me
(even I know hope exists)
central park ran out of
squirrel's in granite
Gotham
where the other 9 million
like me endure or triumph over
life
their voices
calling near
and far
for salvation
out of the darkness
one more yesterday
competing for a prize

Escape Road

few weeks ago
the river ran green
I had not a care in the world
fish swam by
caught on the fly
by and by

then the rain came
I went back to work
all the cares came running home
who wants what
when do they want it

in my mind's eye
the river still is green
(in reality it is brown, muddy)
it is where I always escape to
even if only in my dreams
the cars keep coming to the garage
waiting to be fixed

I am off somewhere
getting another part
dreading the return
yet
all is as all is
one day at a time

fishing
or
fixing cars

I live
I breathe
I care

don't go away mad
just go away

bicyle poem

second speed up hill
gears in orbit
bent down
drop forged
double butted
iron tubed
two wheel
wonder
o sunshine
o rain o music
a silent
thank you

Person or Person's Unknown

why
do I
lie
what makes me not tell the truth
even
when I know what I have to say
is perfectly good enough
without embellishments
yet when faced I turn
and create an answer from dust
about the most trivial things
where I went
who I saw
what I said

this part of my makeup
requires some attention
it will get its due
then
I
will be a better man

Close no Cigar

crest fallen
caught alone again
running to the shelter of the keyboard
tapping out a plea for company
not external but to connect inside

keeping inside what hides outside
the truth of my nature
afraid at odds with myself
these words offer the medication
my soul needs to say what I mean

it has been pointed out to me
much of what I say is to entertain
instead of the heart song
speak the truth
the truth speaks the heart song
never wonder about the truth
the heart song never lies

Penny Wise

empty handed empty headed
alone at night
calling in a voice
softly
where is the next poem
the mood
the season
the river
the darkness

promise of love
photograph memories
sunlight in the garage
holding her hand
my grandsons
the everyday up and down of things

all this and more
await the keystroke
sitting alone late at night
awaiting the next inspiration
or a single word to start with

Symptoms

never more far away
right here
where I am sitting
all my life I heard the same things
over and over
what potential
you could go so far

yea I've gone
never more far away
not sure where I belong
if I do at all
the book tells me
(the blue one)
I am restless, irritable, discontent
those are some of the symptoms
selfish self centered self seeking
suffering the delusion I can be like other people

never more far away
when
I look in the mirror

When

the last night
    long vigil
by the window
    nearly killed
me

this night
control is present
yet
I am not happy

what answer do I hope
    darkness produces
hour by hour
    in stillness
aware
seconds
minutes
still frame TV

show pictures not invented
        when does the vision
begin
when
does the day
begin

Broadway (frisco)
210 am

Carlos
still searches
Shannon's shadow
along Eddy street
   in doorways
    on corners
neon cafés

rare is love
when
it's ass
for profit
abundant
unhappy
side effects

Broadway (frisco)
210 am

Saturday Sunday
   late march

near the end of another run
some bitter powder left
rowdy hells angels pass
I remain aloof
spending hours like
money
Dominic
such a beautiful
name
who am I
when will this
all
end

Here is this cold march morning, a little after 8, headed up the stairs at the Hall of Justice, to face the grim beginning

chase ideas for a dime
one line at a time
knowing what I know now
go back to
Viet Nam in underpants
than walk up those stairs

who possibly in any right mind
turns them self in
but
to run
only makes it worse
they will catch you
it always happens

how bad can prison be
can't cook you
can't eat you
won't shoot you
less you run

o
well
once you're in the door
the sunlight is over
or the darkness begins
don't be so melodramatic

it is only time
I am still young
take notes,
there will be a test

life takes some pretty
strange turns
this day and age
listen
just put it on the page

Folsom Dam

when I was
in prison
I had a job
in the graveyard
old convicts
buried
un marked
forgotten

for three years
I numbered
cleared every grave
between 1919 to 1978
two hundred souls
were laid to rest
I never saw their faces
or hear their voices
yet I know all their names

now some fifteen years
later
it is a part of who I am
we are all connected
in some what or way
even
when we
pass away

Gone Starker

affecting accents
shtick my wife calls it
beating around the mental bush
busted
disgusted
not to be trusted

reading book after book
hiding from my grandsons
smoking cheap cigars
locked out of my own life

even naps don't help
I am in here somewhere
battling inner demons
for a glimpse of the surface
underwater I am
in the cesspool of my own negativity

and the next day
wait for the mail
hoping for an envelope full of hope
or a bit of the dole

it will get better
soon as I confess
all my sins,
pray with my heart not my mouth
break water
sail again free as daylight
in God's own hands

Monastic

but just
praying all the
time and
fasting
doing a drop out
cover up
is less than
perfect
we need to
explore
not abuse
or neglect
each other
these days years days years
shit is fast
and furious
all complicated
full of data
mega feedback
radio wave spider webs
moral minefields
candles
on the altar

La Gloria

coffee and a cigar
early Friday morning
waiting for the final edit
the changes
the changes
that need to be made
life
is just like
poetry
yet
the lines break
where life says
not where the
poet
puts them   this is a new year
                                could this be a new man

waiting for the edit
let the mercy of
God
move my heart
and help me end
with grace

Thinking Again

work
    read
go fish
chase ideas across
paper
on empty

bop up Taylor street
check bay bridge panorama
favorite vision
corners
a slice of sky
over concrete
green water passin
wander from
one bridge to the other
San Francisco
morning
glad
for another day

Subway Cars

in transit
sitting still
moving inside million miles an hour
catch fleeting glimpses
times gone by
writing, waiting, being uncertain
a one page review
all the time gone by
what was wasted
nothing
it was all collected
now
overwhelmed by mental vastness
the outline
the content
all in between
when what l want
is to have it figured
it does not compute
the amount is correct
the bill is written on the wrong paper

muddled be fuddled chasing the ghost
of all the old poems
looking for the new voice
but saying the same thing
this is the challenge
am I up to the task
only time will tell

Grumpy

when you do
reflect
on America
the super bowl
this greedy
nowhere worthless
Godless
goofy side show
in public
   while so many
worthy servants
of
God all mighty and each other
go naked
underfed

it's all kinda outaoder
I'll just
get a glass of water
and go to bed

to cook a pot of rice

such a simple, elegant food
feeding the body
mining the soul

after the water boils away
reminds me of what is
left after a dream

awake, haunted, memories flash by
what was she singing

the sameness of the days
   is beginning to wear on me
like old shoes, too long kept

distracted, out of reach
   uninterested in anything
watching my life, leak away

obsess fishing, smoking giant cigars
   drinking way too much coffee
unable to focus, or pray

it has been so long since I had an original thought
   I fear never having one again
I go to the movies

I can't even escape there
   this is a prison without walls
I have locked myself in

I wonder if
  it is really
possible
to stand by +
observe
my downfall, again
da rent
the wages
the stolen all
go up my nose
bitter memory of
25 years old
and the first bouts of
self destruction

```
o dear
      I fear
            falling
steps taken
          slowly
a case of the jitters
                the demons no longer
                            whisper
they jump right up and shout
we got you by the neck
doing all they can
not to let me out

I call I call
        deep out of somewhere
          alone, late at night
o dear God help me
give me strength
to fight

this is more than sickness
over the line into madness
don't know to call the doctor
or just
lay down and die
my nose bled all over the underwear she left in the truck
using the center line
to navigate my way
home
over crosswalk, stopping
        at the light
that crazy woman and I
took such a chance with our life
```

last year I crossed a line
better not gone over
lost weeks, got sick, took my punishment
like I need to

in the face of another calendar gone
broken promise or not
this is a new year
for what hours
left to writing, need taken
for what hours left to working
a time to sleep, eat, read be quiet

facing the real possible facts
I am dishonest
I do not do what I need to do, to live sober
even without using,
this talent I have been given, is slipping away

clear thought
careful wording
poetry with craftsmanship
say what needs saying
leave the rest in a pile of broken dreams

with one breath I tell
myself
it is just a bunch of boards nailed together
brick fronted, on green grounds
in another gasp
this is my home
I have been here, long time now
the walls have seen me bleed
my best words escaped into the garage night

not to mention the woman I live here with
not lain together for years
bitter tension, passing inconsistency
each rooted stubborn neither one correct
both half wrong

I must walk away
    (what I learned to do from my parents)
tears, fears, justifiable confusion
washing away the best time I have ever known
yet
my God is big
he will take me, there must be
more than boards nailed together
brick fronted on green grounds
double sad,
expectations, are resentments
under construction

had to cry out
    roar across the phone line
no more my friend, it is going to kill me

past all reason, completely helpless
    in the grip, of my own destruction
      before there were limits, money, time, connections

faced with abundant supply, bags of cash
    no restrictions of movement
this deadly dance is horrific

there is only one possible ending
    that sure seems likely
        dead in days
at the melting point
    toxic, deranged, unable to stop
              o God what have I gone and done
            again

miscreants malefactors muggers
side show strongmen
dope fiends
wish to be gangsters
make believe fools

show me your companions
I will show you who you are
a long ago nun's voice echoes
up the cellblock a con's voice echoes
come chow time I be tagging that ass
alone in the cell wondering
who's ass be tagged

square barred window gives off light
over head bulb on all night
a trustee mops the catwalk
for the tenth time that day
another many years to go

I have read the bible
cover to cover fifty times this year
the clatter of cups the rattle of keys
chow time is here

when and if I go
I am not coming back

who will lay a flower
on my grave
where will I be remembered
when this poison kills me
as it sure will
who will dress my
corpse
carry my casket
bid me be gone
not the most pleasant
thoughts
here Tuesday night
in December
all it took was one bad
decision
off the chart
instantly
bag after bag after bag
chasing oblivion
escape my own
torment
with madness
night after night
bag after bag

anyone reading
this notebook
gets free admission
to my turmoil
bouncing off the baseboards
climbing up
stairways
in and out of focus
with other deserted
souls
share lost causes
of bizarre needle
bad light collapsed veins
melodramas
the one who could be
my sister
the other half of me
in female form
she has her own tangled
web of sadness
witness to her last tragedy
the shadow man
helps her
with a rig full of decay
to the neck

out night walking again
              despite all the past proof
this can only lead to another downfall
the company of street lights windows passing traffic
the same empty stare I always have when in
this condition
where does the road start to turn   home ward
    who will wait up for me
         no person calls me in
               some comfort or company
alone with bad habits taking no safe
    direction in search of more oblivion
         there is no one who waits
             or wonders when this will end

take a close look around the full view does not include a return ticket, the train has left without me I go on asking other unseen faces what does the end really look like

opium in bed
  on easter Sunday
Christ
     should be
          risen by now

  I have to go
      downstairs
and let him out

soon another calendar will
live out its time
add another number
write another line
winds of winter
ice on the glass
up jumped the devil
kicked me in the ass
if I was not at the church
he would have got me by the neck
trembling, terrified of going back
all the alleys
the doorways
dark eyes of evil
peddling tastes of this or that
road to ruin
take the next right
death, destructions despair
further on ahead
stay here, pray for protection
deliver me from madness
all I was
is, still me
waiting for permission
to fall towards darkness
out, alone, in the company
of the wolf
who wants my soul

don't have enough days left
to waste any
on cars
other people's dreams
pay attention to what is
not what seems

every day I ask God
to help me stay sober
the rest
is up to me
less time left, than gone
the break down puzzles me
days weeks hours
make the minutes count
the rest will come to heel

not what I think
what I feel
this world is inviting
with material gift
that snare is just a trap
if just for today
I do my best
God
will do the rest

can't seem to trust a lot
these days
my faith
fragile
as my grip on reality

making my own measure
the ruler is so short
maze blaze barbed wire
fence line between confidence
sitting in the chair, doing nothing
thinking nothing, lost alone afraid

so unlike me
my brash loud har har self
inside I am falling apart
a dozen different ways at once

get a grip old boy
put one foot in front of the other
march on
make this unhappy time be
gone

all the effort
went out the window
never stopped to ponder
how bad it could get
well be advised
this is awful
no more room to
disappear in
the watch keeper
counts days
by computer
the man upstairs
senses some
disturbance
in my behaviors
all the while chasing
the connections
eight ball after eight ball
my whole life
goes
down the sewer

words escape
into air
instead of on
paper

clean room
engine assembly
German, Italian, English
sealed surface
mated
new gasket perfect
careful measure
tolerance, clearance
run out
end play
work
max results
the real reward
wages, or flat rate
work is work

God bless it

out alone
    after midnight
alley way of the deserted soul
pacing between doorways
      around the echo chamber
of my wheezing heart
other sadness terror
    spirit breaking voices
longer walks at
later still hours
accompanied with invisible
demonic henchman
all along the river side
no one sees my going
there is no safe sidewalk
or destination
in sight

we will see what
the dawn at work
delivers
as I stumble in
bleary
dazed dejected
all self control erased
no sign of Dominic
only his shadow
              in and out
              of the bathroom
              up and down the
              halls
not still
for one minute
who does he think he
is kidding
it is just a matter of
hours
before someone
sends me to pee
              in the bottle

what it seems like
    there was not enough value
placed on my sobriety
what times I did be glad for
    all had something to do with recovery

what do I really care about
    where does this pure self destruction
come from
was the safe clean life too easy
    did it really take a stroke of genius
   to toss so many years in the scrap heap
willing to be beaten by the same old nasty drip of frenzy

don't call my name
  I am underground
not to surface any time soon
lost with no
particular reason, it is the most natural of states
for addicts to be in
up, chasing, collapsed, up chasing again
what is really amazing, not one part of this changed
a bit the cost is still deadly
the effects of it all are still
disaster

got a good job
    great location
respect, responsibility, rewards
it all could go up in powder
if I don't stop now
      there is no other outcome
but failure, rejection
    unemployment
even I don't believe
    they are fooled
how many days can
pass
utterly distracted
do head colds really last
      weeks
can this be explained away
with
smoke and mirrors
we think now
      if it don't get better
tomorrow
it is not going to
out on my ass again
laid out played
out
totally defeated

the night demons still
call to me

April full moon Friday
but I am more of a sunlight
person now
wonder what ever happened
to my side shift knucklehead
or the dirty jeans I once proudly wore

whisper more than call
fishing beats fast bikes any day
regrets about the past
not many
I was foolish

not wise yet
just less foolish, more carefully
aware less concerned about what was
more hopeful of what might be

when this batch
        of run over days nights
does finally close curtain
the cost is not in numbers
        it's in heartbeats
reduction of hours, sunsets
all that is left
        causes me much discomfort
nerves that were steel cable
unraveled
strand by strand
exposed raw tender
        repeat effect abuse brings
what little safe space
        left
closing all the windows
doors to other refuge locked with
no way to enter
then take another hit
   jolt of electric current
over wires overloaded long ago
the notebook took ten days to fill up
this December   while 18 years
of effort, did not count
deductions will be made from total time left
                              desperate for affection
bent over in toxic spasms becoming another
doomed long night walker

in the space of one week
I have undone years of effort
all for some bitter shit I hate
but can't stop using once it gets started
went along alright after separating
took pretty good care of myself
then in a moment of out of focus thinking
there I was
where I always wind up when I do dope

dumb disgusted deranged in a nose dive
not like it took major crime unit
to figure,
for a few weeks I been loopy
took no action
left my self open
up jumped my old friend self destruction
we got in the car together
been out here ever since

Monday evening
   lasted until 4pm
Wednesday finish of
the worst episode ever
      enough is enough
three lines left
on the mirror
blew them out the doorway

ask all the power of Heaven
to make it stop now
not at 3am, or next week
in this very moment
I surrender, there is no possible
way to defeat this demon past
adventures prove it the future depends
   on it
    at the end it all comes back to this
     blood, bad breath, cloudy eyed, complete state
of pain

this will not
end easy
all my own devices
can't stop me
there is splat
        slap
        slam
        dump
        down
coming
time real soon here
cry for help
could save me
then the phone rang
slick as silk on soft shoulders
lied my way
into two more eight balls
son, you got to get a grip
the room is beginning to spin
in orbit
trembling insides perfectly
matching
all my congested airwaves
completely knowing
this is suicide

better take refuge
in the shed
while it is still safe
to do so
there are noises of
    who and why
do you know what
    hours he keeps
why some time he is in there
two days sleeping
then
only tire tracks
    or footprints on the shower floor
be careful Dominic
      the pain
      is really causing you
      to come apart
all over
eyes ears nose throat

what ever is so obvious
for some of these people
who have seen my second
    skin ego
do a dark walk of silence
    could become, soon
common knowledge

demons depart
    take the dark shadow off
    my doorway
go infect some other lost soul
leave me alone
my voice cracking
vision cloudy
unseen forces
tearing pieces of my heart apart
I let them
as if
this were just a detour
on the road to
damnation
little faith left
must sustain me
as I cry out
in utter
desperation
o God make this the last
death watch
be over, call me out
from under
set me free from my own
torment

at risk again
late alone
loaded
November remember
periodically sends
me
chasing
shadows, streetlamps
leafless branches
into the wasteland of my
soul
even in the best of times
I yearn for
disaster

making noise early in Church
groaning before God
stop me
before
I die

I do not enjoy mystery
like I once did
sounds of my empty
heart
solitude internal
sixty years old
on my way to
emptiness

walk by the church
see icons of
saints looking down at me
I tremble
they know what desperate dark forces
are in me leading
into this pit of personal tragedy

    the years of ground care
               many mowing hours
hours spent here
safe and free
  of my malady
then at all hours of the night days on end
in passing the faces of the Saints
see my soul go so
willingly in the grasp of
the wolf
where else is left for me to escape to
what other choice do I have
if this goes on any longer

    the rest of what little bit
      I achieved here
will go to dust with no refund
take these eyes out of my head
      still the ache inside me
          show me how to serve again
not be led to slaughter
              breathing gagging waiting for the end

was I bored
        unhappy
unable to cope with everyday routine
even when I looked so content on my bucket with a cigar
        work was going well
I got promoted, put on salary
was even producing, showing some skill talent overall competence
did I have a hidden painful secret
                was the marriage ending
more than I could bear

that afternoon I left for San Francisco
        there were no warning signs
had lots of money, nice clothes
the depth of my insane other identity, let loose
        on a walk in Oakland
under the BART tracks, panting, unable to breathe
sweat, chills completely controlled
        dose by dose
by the time I got to Mary's house it was
too late, the voice the eyes the constant
motion, gave it all away
        if I ever had a day to do over
I never would have caused her such discomfort
        back to Oregon
defeated, with no more shameful act
to follow that one, just kept falling
Nov 20 to Dec 17, days of disorder
no focus
what came before, is no matter
it is all about
how I recover

return of the smiley eyed next door honey blond
we wile away the rest of the afternoon without
costing anybody anything
ideas clear on one sunny afternoon write a story
on the garage called the way we were
every car passing that's the one
a sly young girl slams out of the house in a rage
about the madness
her wild eyes move in
a motion known only to her

the next door lady goes home
I count the numbers of faces
a six man stolen car ring
on coney island
and the story never gets
on paper

did I really
        live with her
for fifteen years
had all the days together
                meant anything
were we ever good to each other
        or always
on each other's nerves
sat here alone, wondering
why did it take so long
        to unravel
was that space I made
        in the garage
really mine
or just cost me every
                paycheck
the seasons
        passed into
some spot distant
departed with no return
of effort
the thing was a big disaster
with me left
bitter, disgusted
at the sight of her

accept the end with some grace
even if the cost was too high

                        the rose
                of gerke alley
is gone back to asia
for good
put all the past in
a paper bag
tossed overboard
mid pacific
wave a final
by by
say bodeo no more
dance dispair for me
not
go
she says
get clever
gear by gear
align
half a step
half a step half a step
more
full face fade out

believe it
the power of the river
having traveled so very far
to get here
even if only to pass

our (all of us) faces
are as different from each other
river bottom stones take eons to make
we are here and already gone
lifetimes mean nothing
to the river

our (all of us) blood
in total would wash by in a week
meet the ocean and turn to salt
overnight
river keeps moving
floods drops rises again
as God did
in His time here

our (all of us)
stand here with me
watch the river go by
thank you (all of us)
make this new day special
it is the only day we have
as the river goes by

By Some Happenstance

a book. a diner, greasy spoon
double urn coffee makers
soggy bagels n a one legged guy name Ernie
my own time at the CHAT N CHEW in Frisco
where the Ernie was name Pat wit an anchor tattoo
provided if any thing a breakfast meal that
would assure one of bowel regularity
if ya made it home on time
wandering thru my book lined room thinking peering
remembering title place story and some of em
(books not authors of) are like old dead pals
ya just dust off and want not yet to bury em
or for simple simons sake donate em to some *cause&effect*
last night was another night in bed alone practicing
being dead
yet, having ground up some KGB blend dark beans
like a mythical sub-human golem to the brew and rise
forgive me miss Plath....I rise like a specter with gray hair
to eat air and
avoid the *social ramble*
cockamamie bullshit by the 6dollar 36cents NY Times Sunday
fish wrap....enduring another walk to the end of Never Land
crap shoot government folly....dis n dat comic book pow zap
kaboom bluster muster salacious salutations abound
over the ruling class...who use deflect and deny
blame every body else......*refer here to messes of my own
making* how ever I do admit when I am wrong
not blame you or lets see
Jews
Blacks
Muslims
Mexicans
Queers

Drugs
Guns
gotdam fucking any body maybe guilty
how ever in that hallowed halo hallway
Mr + Mrs Billy Bolla n a dolla factory
never get a taste of revenge resist or refer to as
slimy ass scam artists who indeed breed upon the
lives of the lower classes
I gonna go back to my *spartan colloquial*
.......in closing let me not forget to say to
all the women on earth
THANK YOU

about the author:

Dominic Albanese was born in Hell's Kitchen three months after the atomic bomb dropped. Gas jockey carney chop-shop soldier mechanic musician radio poet. Mixed up with life and its characters. A sharp observer and participant. He retired gone fishin' on the Treasure Coast. And always always poetry.

www.ingramcontent.com/pod-product-compliance
Lightning Source LLC
Chambersburg PA
CBHW020145130526
44591CB00030B/218